C000062540

# YOSEMITE

## THE CYCLE OF THE SEASONS

ONE TREE, THREE SEASONS

and Jim Wilson
Graphic Design by Jeff Nicholas

Layout and graphic design performed on a
Macintosh® SE utilizing Aldus PageMaker®
and Aldus Freehand®. All texts set in Palatino
and Optima Typefaces by MacinType,
Fresno, Ca. Color separations and printing
coordinated by Interprint, Petaluma, Ca.

Printed in Hong Kong

First Edition 1990
Second Edition 1991

SIERRA PRESS, INC.

P.O. BOX 25, EL PORTAL, CA. 95318

We wish to thank Len McKenzie, Chief Park
Naturalist, his dedicated staff and the National
Park Service and its employees, both past and
present. It is due to their foresight and hard
work that wonderlands such as Yosemite are
still here for each of us to enjoy. It is up to each
of us, as individuals, to make certain our own
use is consistent with the long-term needs of
these natural temples.

*This book is dedicated
to those who stop;*

*to see, to hear, to smell, to taste, to feel,*

*not just to know,
but to understand*

# YOSEMITE

## THE CYCLE OF THE SEASONS

## CONTENTS

# INTRODUCTION

There are few places on earth which so stirs the soul as Yosemite National Park. Whether seen from the summit of a 13,000-foot peak in the backcountry or viewed through the sun-dappled shade of a riverside cottonwood in Yosemite Valley, this is a land of superlatives. Half Dome, Tuolumne Meadows, El Capitan, these landmarks are as well known in Europe and Asia as they are in America.

Since its 'discovery' in 1851, Yosemite's beauty has attracted painters, writers and photographers . Thomas Moran and Alfred Bierstadt were so overwhelmed they were led to gross overstatement. John Muir spent much of his life attempting to capture in words some fleeting semblance of this landscape. Fiske, Watkins and Muybridge brought back vivid evidence of this landscape's wonders, triggering the tide of visitors who would follow to see, experience and discover for themselves, this glorious work of Nature.

Today's visitors, be they artists or seekers of beauty, owe a great debt to these first adventurers. Without their dedication and perseverance our national parks might not exist today. Considered by many to be the 'crown jewels' of the American landscape, our national parks are much more than landmarks and infinitely more than mere curiosities. They are, rather, refuges of the human spirit; landscapes against which one can measure one's self. We are reminded of our own insignificance and at the same time of our oneness with all life. Muir said that the closer one looked, the more linked all life is with all other life, and this includes us.

It was not so long ago in the history of mankind, that 'wild' places were the norm, not the exception. It is not surprising that great energy was expended in taming these 'wild' places, in converting them to our use, transforming them to our needs. The nineteenth century poet, Walt Whitman, wrote:

*".....the earth is rude, silent, incomprehensible at first; Nature is rude and incomprehensible at first; be not discouraged, keep on, there are divine things well envelop'd, I swear to you there are divine things more beautiful than words can tell."*

Today, this 'rude, silent, incomprehensible'

Nature is cherished. We travel great distances and exert great energy to see what is left of these 'wild' places. Many consider these places sacred, more important for what they are than for any use mankind might make of them. The individual who takes the time and exerts the energy to really 'see' these places learns more about him or herself than anything else.

Today's first-time visitor to Yosemite will most assuredly be overwhelmed by the grandeur of the landscape. Towering monoliths and thundering waterfalls are irresistible sirens vying for our attention. Ultimately, however, one's attention is drawn to the more 'mundane'; the texture of granite, the pattern of pine needles strewn on the forest floor, the sighing of an afternoon breeze as it passes through meadow grasses, "divine things more

hidden treasures that abound. We hope this book will act as a catalyst to memory and as an insight into one's self. Finally we ask that you share these beauties and insights with your friends, your neighbors, and especially your children so that they too might better understand the importance of our continued vigilance and hard work to preserve such "rude, silent, and incomprehensible" places.

Finally, we would like to thank all those local photographers who shared their work with us , so that we might share it with you, the reader. This spirit of sharing, this generosity of vision, has greatly enriched our appreciation of this natural wonder, as we are sure it will yours.

So now, sit back, turn the page, and enjoy....... Yosemite, the Cycle of the Seasons.

# WINTER

*I* wish you were here, for Yosemite is an avenue of beauty and tranquility. From lush valley meadows, to thunderous waterfalls, from peace in the high country, to stunning granite massifs. All its splendors, great and small, captivate your entire being and allow your mind to drift into a zone of nonexistent time.

*L*isten—for today is the first day of Winter and it is hushed by the sound of nothing. Silently, soft, white puffs of heaven-sent manna quilt the earth. Snow flocked black oaks starkly contrast the pure white fluff resting on their dark branches. The air is clean and crisp, bearing the frigid fragrance of fresh frozen vapor.

Occasionally the silence is broken by frolicsome coyote pups, playfully yipping and crunching the crystaline meadows as they toss and roll about, or the whispering of deer as they browse through snow to find the cache of Autumn's stubble. And suddenly, during a rare moment, cloaked in the powder-blue fog of predawn, comes a chilling prehistoric croak of a great blue heron as it lifts from a frozen pond.

Against the lapis sky of Winter's midmorn, a muffled plopping sound echoes across the valley floor as sunstruck trees drop their snowy burden on the unsuspecting. Ruddy cheeks and icy moustaches uplift and are warmed by the hovering orb while backs stay chilled from its diminished rays.

Still, deep in sleepy shadows, are icy dreams of days gone by and glaciers yet unborn.

INCENSE-CEDAR, WINTER

VALLEY VIEW, WINTER MOONRISE

FRESH SNOW, EL CAPITAN MEADOW

WINTER REFLECTIONS ON THE MERCED RIVER

BRIDALVEIL FALL FROM TUNNEL VIEW

HALF DOME FROM HIGHWAY 41

EL CAPITAN, WINTER SUNSET

MERCED RIVER, FIRST SNOW

EL CAPITAN, WINTER

MERCED RIVER, WINTER MORNING

OAK BRANCHES OVER EL CAPITAN

ROCKS, ICE AND SUNSET LIGHT

# S P R I N G

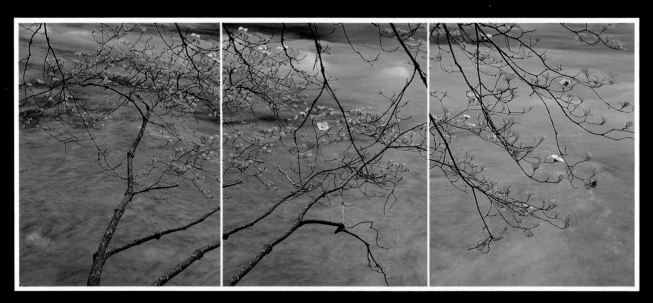

DOGWOOD OVER THE MERCED RIVER

Listen, for today is the first day of Spring. Mating migrators offer daybreak songs of love as they delicately prepare for the advent of new life. Gentle showers moisten faces as warm breezes dry them off. Trees rustle in the wind. Fruit blossoms intoxicate the air and rivers first taste the now liquid snow.

Lime-green leaves unfurl overnight and fecund meadows ooze with the thawing of Winter. There is a light scent of decay as nutrients prepare for the coming rebirth, even the earthbound fog carries the musty odor. Snow laden peaks melt into thundering waterfalls plummeting fluid comets to the quaking earth. Treetop babes brazenly cry to be fed while discarded pinecones from hungry squirrels bounce limb to limb with a final thump on the needle-carpeted floor.

Perfumed foothills trade snowflake for blossom and a distinct bouquet from flower painted roadsides welcomes in the season. Emerald meadows are hued with butterflied horizons while droning bees dance atop wild Iris. Yellow banners of heady scented tree pollen wave across the heavens while the fresh aroma of new grass and the smell of spearmint spices the Valley floor.

Water splashes in boulder strewn rivers, and twittering Ouzels dip into the rapids. Chirping crickets and croaking frogs line the raging shores to harmonize with the aquatic song while high above, soaring on unseen thermals, birds of prey write silent lyrics across the sky.

In the still of night, the massive, jagged brow of Half Dome is graced with a myriad of brilliant stars. Warm moonlit walks reveal hidden faces in stone, yellow blossoms of Evening Primrose and drenching mists from forever high falls are crowned with a lunar rainbow.

YOSEMITE FALLS

GOLDEN POPPIES, MERCED RIVER CANYON

WILDCAT FALLS

SNOW PLANT AND LICHENS

HALF DOME, ORCHARD

AVALANCHE CREEK

SHOWY MILKWEED

CATHEDRAL ROCK AND SPIRES

MISTY BASE OF NEVADA FALL

DOGWOOD ALONG THE MERCED RIVER

POND LILIES, SIESTA LAKE

DOGWOOD AND DOUGLAS-FIR

COOK'S MEADOW

LUPINE LEAVES AND PINE NEEDLES

BRIDALVEIL FALL AND THREE GRACES

CORN LILY AND MONKEYFLOWER, SUMMIT MEADOW

# SUMMER

TENAYA LAKE

*Listen, for today is the first day of Summer. Thunder echoes between the grandiose walls. Lightning illuminates the blackened sky with its blinding flash of energy and wisps of rain from a passing cloud tap glisten the granite to a wet silver-gray.*

*Strong, long and mighty, the sun no longer hides its warmth in shadow. Summer leaves, green with chlorophyll, gather strength to bear fruit. Tender babes of the earth begin to venture on their own. Youthful beldings peek from earthen holes. Fledgling grosbeaks frantically flap as they hit the ground with a graceless thunk. Spotted fawns play chase the butterfly and tiny trout make heroic leaps for the prized fly.*

*Misty rainbows and the balm of ozone provide refreshment on steep trails to lofty peaks. Here, high in the alpine, glorious bouquets decorate the barren slopes with splashes of intense color. Sun warmed rocks and an ancient breeze become ideal companions for an afternoon nap.*

*Yearning for peace, we find solitude in the alpine. A haven to draw within oneself, void of the ticking we gauge our lives by. The tranquility of the wilderness draws us into a relaxed state of mind. Everything a complement to everything else, we realize, we too, are a complement of nature.*

*Here we rest.*
*Here we gain.*
*The expanse.*
*The serenity.*

*The absolute quiet of the high country.*

BLACK OAKS IN COOK'S MEADOW

EVENING PRIMROSE, EL CAPITAN MEADOW

JEFFREY PINE ON SENTINEL DOME

LUPINE AND PEARLY EVERLASTING ALONG THE TIOGA ROAD

GIANT SEQUOIAS

DEER GRAZING IN EL CAPITAN MEADOW

SUNSET AT TUNNEL VIEW

BRACKEN FERN AND RED CONE

GREAT GRAY OWL

CLOCKWISE: MULE DEER, COYOTE, STELLER'S JAY

CLIMBERS ON ELEPHANT ROCK

LIGHTNING STORM FROM OLMSTED POINT

HALF DOME FROM OLMSTED POINT

JUNIPER AND GRANITE

TUOLUMNE MEADOWS, UNICORN PEAK

CATHEDRAL LAKE AND PEAK

POOL NEAR OLMSTED POINT

TARN IN DANA MEADOW, MAMMOTH PEAK

HIGH COUNTRY POOL

LEMBERT DOME, TUOLUMNE MEADOWS

HEATHERS AT VOGELSANG

MT. HOFFMAN, SUNSET

SUNSET ON LODGEPOLE PINES, TUOLUMNE MEADOWS

UNICORN PEAK, TUOLUMNE MEADOWS

AUTUMN

Listen, for today is the first day of Autumn. Squirrels begin preparing for Winter and a feverish pitch of gathering takes dominion over their day. Dried leaves rustle about as they bury even more acorns. With cheeks bulging, they scamper into the earth and ready their warm winter's nest. They fatten and add a thicker, more luxurious coat.

In the early light of dawn, beneath a blanket of wispy fog, the meadows sleep. Last night's campfire smoke still lingers in the air. Summer dissolves before our eyes and memories of Autumns past cloud the present.

There is a departure of green from the leaves as chlorophyll retreats. Hemp threads the meadows with gold, while Dogwoods, Maples, and Oaks add to the incredible brilliance. Once again the Valley becomes a kaleidoscope of colors.

Afternoon gusts sweep the dried branches and showers of multi-hued leaves tinkle from above. Swirling winds corral the bristling display and gently rest them on sleepy ground. At dusk, El Capitan sparkles with climbers' flashlights as they bid the slumbering Valley good-night. Save for the repeated howl of coyotes baying at the moon, there is an absence of woodland sounds. Rings of fire fill the chill of twilight with a smokey aroma and campers huddle to glowing embers as the cool of night draws near.

Days shorten and even the mighty icons reach to the sun with a warm glow of gold. Waterfalls slow to a trickle and the river becomes a meandering current of multi-colored leaves.

LEAVES IN FERN SPRING

HALF DOME, AUTUMN ALPENGLOW

INDIAN HEMP, MERCED RIVER

CASCADE FALLS

AUTUMN FOLIAGE, HIGH COUNTRY

SIESTA LAKE

BIGLEAF MAPLE BLOWING IN AN AUTUMN BREEZE

YOSEMITE FALLS FROM STONEMAN MEADOW

COTTONWOOD ALONG THE MERCED RIVER

AUTUMN FOLIAGE

RIVULET AND LEAF MOSAIC

HALF DOME, AUTUMN AFTERNOON

AUTUMN MORN, MERCED RIVER

INCENSE-CEDAR, AUTUMN FOLIAGE

FOG AND FOREST FLOOR

REFLECTIONS AND MAPLE LEAVES

# WINTER

## A BRIEF REPRISE

SUNSET, EL CAPITAN

OLMSTED POINT, CLEARING STORM

LAST LIGHT, YOSEMITE VALLEY

SKIER AT SUNSET, YOSEMITE HIGH COUNTRY

*Listen— for today is the first day of Winter and it is hushed by the sound of nothing. I wish you were here, to share in the warm benedictions of these seasons. To be moved by Nature's rhythm, captured in her zone of non-existent time. And upon parting, allowing the "whole" of Yosemite's treasures, to become your mind's secret hiding place.*

# INTERPRETIVE NOTES ON THE PHOTOGRAPHS

**Cover: Half Dome, Autumn Sunset.**

**10. Incense-cedar, Winter.** This cinnamon-barked tree played an important role for early inhabitants of the Sierra Nevada. Indians used the thick, fibrous bark to fashion huts called 'u-mu-chas' while pioneers used it for roofing. John Muir also admired them for their shelter, "In its prime, the whole tree is thatched with (beautiful fern-like plumes).....so that they shed off rain and snow like a roof, making fine mansions for storm-bound birds and mountaineers".

**11. Valley View, Winter Moonrise.** Prior to the establishment of the one-way road system, visitors entering from the north would first see Yosemite Valley from this viewpoint, thus its alternative name, 'Gates of the Valley'. Earlier, horse-bound visitors knew this viewpoint as 'Rocky Ford'.

**12. Fresh Snow, El Capitan Meadow.** Meadows slumber beneath a blanket of winter snow against the backdrop of 'The Acorn', a side formation to Cathedral Rock. Snow, so familiar in small scale, can become an overpowering, earth-shaping force when amassed in glacial form. Once filling the valley from rim to rim, successive waves of glaciation have scoured the valley many times in the past million years.

**13. Winter Reflections on the Merced River.** As if by magic 'mirrors of water' can reduce the giant monoliths to manageable proportions. Time spent wandering the obscure, calm bends of the Merced River will return abundant memories of peace and serenity.

**14. Bridalveil Fall From Tunnel View.** The Ahwahnechee Indians called this waterfall, Pohono, apparently after a group of Miwok Indians called Pohonichi. Translations of unknown origin indicate that Pohono meant puffing, swirling or evil wind. Local Indians believed strongly in this superstition, possibly due to a tragic occurence, and avoided the area in and about the base of Bridalveil Fall.

**15. Half Dome From Highway 41.** The winter season brings a calm to Yosemite Valley. Most animals and birds migrate to warmer locales or bed down while the meadows turn dormant. Clouds often swirl the brow of Half Dome, hiding its face for hours and, from time to time, days.

**16. El Capitan, Winter Sunset.** El Capitan, 'the chief or the captain', is composed of the oldest and hardest granite in Yosemite Valley. It was originally formed some 140 million years ago and is the tallest 'unbroken' cliff in the world, rising 3,245 feet above the meadows at its base.

**17. Merced River, First Snow.** Originating among the snowfields of Yosemite's southern high country, the Merced River descends more than 11,000 feet in its quest of the sea. Its present name is considerably shorter than that originally conferred, *El Rio de Nuestra Senora de la Merced*, The River of Our Lady of Mercy.

**18. El Capitan, Winter.** When frosted with ice and snow, and wreathed in streamers of fog, El Capitan appears unclimbable. Yet in 1958 it was first scaled by a three man team. It took the trio 45 days, spread over a period of eighteen months, to complete the climb. Today El Capitan is literally covered with climbing routes, attracting climbers from around the globe to attempt what is now, on average, a four day climb.

**19. Merced River, Winter Morning.** Meadows and streamsides slumber under a fresh blanket of snow. Memories of these infrequent and serene winter spectacles are not soon forgotten by those fortunate enough to be here at the right time.

**20. Oak Branches Over El Capitan.** Delicate snow flakes settle on the bare branches of Yosemite's black oaks forming a lace-like pattern. A supreme delight of winter morning visitors is admiring a forest of black-branched trees adorned with millions of miniscule white flakes.

**21. Rocks, Ice and Sunset Light.** Water, whether in liquid or frozen state, has played a major role in shaping the Yosemite we see today. During cooler times, in eons past snowfall gathered and formed massive ice fields. Weight and gravity worked to move these glaciers downward from the Sierra crest, scouring canyons and shaping granitic formations. Our climate has gradually warmed so today the most common ice forms observed are in lakes and rivers during the winter season.

**24. Yosemite Falls.** Shown here during maximum spring melt, Yosemite Falls cascade 2,425 feet creating a thunderous roar echoing throughout the eastern end of the Valley. Run-off from a small portion of Yosemite's northern high country feeds Yosemite Creek. This creek leaps the brink of two sheer cliffs, separated by a tumbling cascade to form the world's fifth highest waterfall.

**25. Golden Poppies, Merced River Canyon.** Each spring, usually in early March, the hillsides of the Merced River Canyon burst forth with the golden orange of two varieties of poppy. The most common is the annual poppy (*Eschscholzia caespitosa*). It is a more diminutive but none-the-less colorful specie, than its larger cousin, the California poppy (*E. californica*). This intensely colorful display usually greets visitors for less than a month each year.

**26. Wildcat Falls.** Wildcat Falls is located west of Yosemite Valley, along Highway 140. Differing from most Park waterfalls, Wildcat Creek cascades down an uneven granite wall, dropping its waters in a series of graceful steps. This characteristic has challenged numerous artists to capture its beauty.

**27. Snow Plant and Lichens.** The blood-red snow plant (*Sarcodes sanguinea*) is a member of the wintergreen family that has no chlorophyll and is incapable of photosynthesis. It can be found growing in the decaying humus of coniferous forests, usually in June and has recently been described as having a mycorrhizal (symbiotic) relationship with fungi.

**28. Half Dome, Orchard.** Rising nearly 5,000 feet above the floor of Yosemite Valley, Half Dome is probably the most recognized 'rock' in America. This glacially carved dome lies between the pathways of two ancient ice flows. Tenaya Canyon, left, and Merced Canyon, right, were carved by two separate glaciers. They joined beneath the dome and,

together, assisted in the formation of the Valley.

**29. Avalanche Creek.** As you drive the Wawona Road, Highway 41, you pass through many creek recesses. In winter they can be treacherous, icy alcoves on an otherwise dry route. During spring and summer these riparian habitats offer wonderful wildflower and shrub displays.

**30. Showy Milkweed.** Of all the beautiful wildflowers in Yosemite, showy milkweed (*Asclepias speciosa*), puts on the longest and most varied show. From May, when it first sprouts a silvery-gray stalk, until October, when the parachute-like seeds are carried in the breeze, their display is astounding. In June, after it has grown a 2- to 4- foot stalk, the delicate, round buds begin to open. These buds form a sphere of many small, pointed, pink flowers.

**31. Cathedral Rock and Spires.** Cathedral Rock is situated directly across the Valley from El Capitan and is composed of similar hard rock. Cathedral Spires are two columns of granite bounded by intersecting vertical fractures. The east spire rises 1,900 feet above the Valley while the east one is 200 feet higher. They were first climbed in 1933 and 1934. The ascent is difficult and recommended only for experienced rock climbers.

**32. Misty Base of Nevada Fall.** Afternoon sun and churning mist create an ethereal landscape easily seen from the Mist Trail above Nevada Fall. This steep, but rewarding, 3.4 mile trail will take the hiker to the top of the Granite Stairway, a glacially carved 'staircase' which includes Vernal, 317 feet, and Nevada, 594 feet, Falls.

**33. Dogwood Along the Merced River.** Hidden deep in the wintry coniferous forests of Yosemite Valley are bare branches awaiting spring. As a new life cycle begins, the western dogwood (*Cornus nuttallii*) bursts forth with creamy-white bracts illuminating the woods with ivory beacons.

**34. Pond Lilies, Siesta Lake.** This aquatic plant can be found in several locations, including Siesta Lake along the Tioga Road. Its large, heart-shaped leaves float lazily on the water's surface. The tight, chalice-shaped yellow blossom never seems to fully open. Pond lilies, due to their ability to root in open water, become an early step in 'meadowization' or 'succession'.

**35. Dogwood and Douglas-Fir.** A favorite of photographers, the dogwood (*Cornus nuttallii*) is a harbinger of spring in the Valley. The 'flowers' are actually bracts with the true blossom being in the center. Small orange-red berries, drupes, will form by early fall. The fruit stage is soon followed by autumn foliage ranging from gold to maroon.

**36. Cook's Meadow.** Park lore tells us that this meadow is known as Cook's Meadow. As early as 1859 visitor services were provided by early entrepreneurs. Included in these services, clustered near and around today's chapel, were photo studios, general store, post office, Park headquarters, saloons, hotels and restaurants. Legend has it that cooks would wander the adjacent meadows during breaks and free time, thus the informal name of Cook's Meadow.

**37. Lupine Leaves and Pine Needles.** The massive icons of Yosemite seem to dominate the attention of most visitors. It is a natural urge to constantly look skyward while admiring the Valley's granite masses but we urge you to occasionally glance at the forest floor. Nature has provided a spectacular, and ever changing, collage of beauty.

**38. Bridalveil Fall and Three Graces.** Bridalveil Fall drops 620 feet from a hanging valley left as glaciers carved away the canyon below. The heavy mists of late-spring and summer create spectacular rainbows on sunny afternoons.

**39. Corn Lily and Monkeyflower, Summit Meadow.** Summit Meadow, along the Glacier Point Road, is a wonderful high country meadow in which to observe Yosemite's colorful wildflowers. The season begins as winter snows recede and continue throughout summer. The moist meadow supports fine displays of camas lily, bistort, monkeyflower, corn lily, tiger lily, shooting star, sneezeweed, death camas and marsh marigold. Across the road are dry land species such as stickseed and lupine.

**42 Black Oaks in Cook's Meadow.** Black Oaks (*Quercus kelloggii*) play an important role in providing a food source for Yosemite's wildlife. Woodpeckers and squirrels work feverishly throughout late summer and fall to stockpile a supply of acorns which will provide for their dietary needs during the long, cold winter.

**43. Evening Primrose, El Capitan Meadow.** This jewel of the wildflower kingdom will put on a show before your very eyes. Its numerous buds open in late evening, and in a matter of a few moments it produces a four-petaled, creamy yellow blossom. The flowers close at daybreak, for it is pollinated solely by the hovering, night-flying hawkmoth.

**44. Jeffrey Pine on Sentinel Dome.** Normally growing to a stately height of over 100 feet, this tree is a classic example of the krummholz effect. Bent in homage to the relentless winds, the contorted remains of this Jeffrey Pine add to this serene and peaceful setting. Sentinel Dome is an easy one mile hike from the parking lot along the Glacier Point Road and from its summit one can place in perspective the overwhelming masses of granite.

**45. Lupine and Pearly Everlasting Along the Tioga Road.** Wildflower displays are one of the greatest delights Yosemite has for visitors. Beginning during February in the foothills and continuing into September in the high country, wildflowers struggle to sprout, bloom and set seed to insure future generations.

**46. Giant Sequoias.** Yosemite's Big Trees, and those of the Sierra, are quite different from the two other species known to exist in the world. Giant sequoia (*Sequoiadendron giganteum*) has a column-like trunk, huge stout branches and its bark is cinnamon-colored. Coastal redwoods (*Sequoia sempervirens*) are taller, more slender and possess a more traditional conifer-like profile. The third specie, dawn redwood (*Metasequoia glyptostroboides*), is indigenous to China.

**47. Deer Grazing in El Capitan Meadow.** Lush meadows at the base of granite icons present the Park's mule deer herds with an abundant supply of forage. Since our national parks provide a sanctuary for all animal species to prosper without interference of mankind, the sight of deer browsing in meadows is quite common.

**48. Sunset at Tunnel View.** This popular viewpoint offers visitors entering from the south, via Highway 41, a truly inspiring introduction to Yosemite Valley. It is not, however, known as Inspiration Point. That location is high above at the site where an earlier road crested the ridge. A short, but steep, trail begins at the south parking area and leads to the true Inspiration Point.

**49. Bracken Fern and Red Cone.** Bracken fern (Pteridium aquilinum) is the most commonly found fern throughout the Sierra Nevada. Its habitat is in moist locations at low elevations and forest floors at higher altitudes, usually to 10,000 feet. Indian hunters were said to favor a diet consisting solely of bracken fiddleheads. They felt their body odor would not alert deer since they too dined on the tender shoots.

**50. Great Gray Owl. 51a. Mule Deer. 51b. Coyote. 51c. Steller's Jay.** Wildlife is an integral part of the natural systems protected in the Park. Please keep a respectful distance from all wildlife so you do not disturb their natural routines. Feeding wild animals is dangerous to visitors, unhealthy for wildlife and it is illegal!

**52. Climbers on Elephant Rock.** Yosemite's great walls and domes attract many hundreds of climbers each year. Here, Chris Falkenstein belays lead climber Ed Barry on Bucket Brigade. Today's climbers strive to accomplish their climbs with a minimum of impact on the environment. They utilize modern, removable hardware that offers maximum protection without scarring the rock.

**53. Lightning Storm From Olmsted Point.** Thunderstorms often bring spectacular rain, lightning and light shows to Yosemite during the hot summer months. In spite of its beauty, a lightning storm can present dangerous and potentially life threatening situations. Check the weather forecast before departing on a hike and be prepared with survival information in the event you are caught on exposed ridges or passes.

**54. Half Dome From Olmsted Point.** Located along the Tioga Road, Olmsted Point offers a wonderful vista down glacially-carved Tenaya Canyon toward Yosemite Valley. Down this creek, large amounts of silt and sand are carried to the Valley each year. It is deposited in what used to be Mirror Lake hastening the process of succession. Mirror Meadow is now rapidly replacing the broad, shallow pool which used to reflect Half Dome and Mt. Watkins.

**55. Juniper and Granite.** The western juniper (Juniper occidentalis) is a gnarled, weather beaten tree found on dry rocky sites of the high country. It has been described as the most picturesque tree in the Sierra, no small accolade considering the competition.

**56. Tuolumne Meadows, Unicorn Peak.** This nearly two-mile long meadow is the largest sub-alpine meadow in the Sierra Nevada. At an elevation of over 8,600 feet, the summer temperatures remain cool, making it a center for camping, climbing and backpacking activities.

**57. Cathedral Lake and Peak.** When time permits but one day-hike from the Tuolumne Meadows area, the destination should be Cathedral Lake. It is a relatively easy eight mile, round trip, hike which includes a modest elevation gain of 1,000 feet. During the height of the glacial epoch Cathedral Peak stood just 200 feet above the ice. While there glance around and imagine what this area looked like under a massive sea of ice.

**58. Pool Near Olmsted Point.** High country wanderers are occasionally surprised and delighted when they happen across an intimate scene like this. A late summer storm approaches a timber-strewn pool and creates another unforgettable moment in Yosemite National Park.

**59. Tarn in Dana Meadow, Mammoth Peak.** The longest 'river of ice' in the Sierra Nevada, the Tuolumne Glacier, had its origin in and around these peaks. From this location it moved primarily in a westward direction, though at times portions probably spilled eastward across Tioga Pass and down Lee Vining Canyon.

**60. High Country Pool.** Tarns, glacially carved depressions in hard granite, catch snow melt and form small pools. Through naturally occurring processes some pools gather soils and eventually sprout grasses and sedges. Wildflowers and shrubs soon follow. Through this process of succession these tarns begin their own eventual demise.

**61. Lembert Dome, Tuolumne Meadows.** Located at the east end of Tuolumne Meadows is a 'roche moutonnee', an unsymmetrical glacier-formed feature. Moving ice crept gradually up its eastern flank, while ripping away huge chunks of granite on the west, thus forming its lopsided profile.

**62. Heathers at Vogelsang.** Mountain *(Phyllodoce breweri)* and alpine heathers *(Cassiope mertensiana)* are but two of the many lovely alpine and subalpine wildflowers found in the Park. They illustrate Nature's ability to adapt to difficult growing conditions. Basic adaptations such as dwarfism, oversized root systems, matting, succulent leaves and red pigmentation allow these hardy plants to complete their life cycle each year.

**63. Mt. Hoffman, Sunset.** Alpine and subalpine areas of the Park can be the most beautiful and, paradoxically, the most inhospitable. Demanding conditions challenge human, animal and plant survival. Incessant winds, abbreviated growing seasons, thin top soil and intense sunlight combine to create a difficult, but rarely impossible, environment.

**64. Sunset on Lodgepole Pines, Tuolumne Meadows.** Lodgepole pine (Pinus contorta var. murrayana) occupies both slopes of the Sierra, usually from 6,500 to 10,500 feet. It is easily distinguished from other Park conifers since it is the only one bearing needles in groups of two. They are unusually stout and short, two inches in length. The cones are shorter still, the smallest, and most plentiful, of western pines.

**65. Unicorn Peak, Tuolumne Meadows.** These lush meadows were the result of a 'little ice age' about 2,500 years ago, which raised the water table and killed the forest that existed at the time. Meandering through the meadows

is the Tuolumne River, whose headwaters originated on the 13,000-foot peaks forming the eastern boundary of the Park.

**68. Leaves in Fern Spring.** Known as the 'smallest waterfall' in Yosemite, Fern Spring is only one of many natural springs in the west end of the Valley. It is the result of a creek high above percolating through the talus slope only to bubble to the surface prior to joining the Merced River. This abundant moisture supports a deciduous forest of dogwood, alder and maple.

**69. Half Dome, Autumn Alpenglow.** Yosemite's most recognizable monolith rises almost 5,000 feet above the Valley to an altitude of 8,842 feet. Cables are put in place each summer to assist hikers up the steep northeast shoulder. The route is steep and strenuous but spectacular views await the persistent.

**70. Indian Hemp, Merced River.** From Pohono Bridge, Indian hemp *(Apocynum cannbinum)* and sunrise combine to create gold and silver glitter along the exposed shoreline of the Merced River. The fiber of this plant was used by the Ahwahnechee people to weave blankets, baskets, rope and fishing line. Its leaves are toxic, but the roots were used as a heart medicine.

**71. Cascade Falls.** The waters of Cascade and Tamarack Creeks join on the sloping granite wall above and then drop approximately 500 feet as Cascade Falls. It joins the Merced River midway through the flat valley known as Cascade Flats. As with others in the Park, Cascade Falls is at its peak in late spring and summer.

**72. Autumn Foliage, High Country.** Due to short growing seasons and a harsh climate the shrubs of the high country tend to be smaller and often form mats which cover large areas of ground. Most commonly seen varieties include mountain ash, thimbleberry, mountain spiraea, mountain heather and Labrador tea.

**73. Siesta Lake.** This pond is another classic reminder of the ability of glaciers to create high country majesty. The low ridge of rocky debris across the Tioga Road is, in reality, a terminal moraine of the cirque glacier that descended from the ridge above. The moraine blocked a small side stream, forming this diminutive lake.

**74. Bigleaf Maple.** Bigleaf maple (Acer macrophyllum) is the only large specie of maple that is indigenous to western North America. An equally appropriate common name for this tree could be 'canyon maple' since, in the southern Sierra, it is largely restricted to moist, shady locations in the deep gorges. According to the U.S.D.A. bigleaf maple produces maple sugar equal to eastern sugar maple in both quality and quantity.

**75. Yosemite Falls from Stoneman Meadow.** Yosemite's numerous waterfalls have been admired since the first people entered this valley. Each summer season Yosemite Falls takes its rightful place as the Park's crown jewel, plummeting 2,425 feet in three segments before coming to rest in the calm stretches of the Merced River.

**76. Cottonwood Along Merced River.** Cottonwood, alder, maple and dogwood flourish along the banks of the Merced River as it meanders through Yosemite Valley. October and November bring a stunning collage of autumn color as chlorophyll retreats from impending winter. This little understood process is triggered by a complex combination of events including shorter days, cooler temperatures and genetic programming.

**77. Autumn Foliage.** In addition to this stunning show the Merced River slows each fall and creates numerous pools and eddies. Uncommonly still waters offer great opportunities to photograph reflections of autumn foliage and Valley icons.

**78. Rivulet and Leaf Mosaic.** Each autumn Nature triggers a complex biological chain of events which leads to a stunning display of color in the leaves of deciduous trees. Americans, for decades, have admired this annual show-of-the-woods from New England to Southern California.

**79. Half Dome, Autumn Afternoon.** Half Dome "is a crest of granite rising to the height of 4,737 feet above the Valley, perfectly inaccessible, being probably the one of all the prominent points about the Yosemite which never has been and never will be trodden by human foot." That bold statement by Josiah Whitney in 1870 held true for only five years, for after weeks of preparatory hole-drilling George Anderson reached the summit on October 12, 1875.

**80. Autumn Morn, Merced River.** Photographers delight in finding colorful reflections in the Merced River. The magical light of sunrise or sunset combine with the big walls of Yosemite Valley to create dramatic images in the water. One need not be a photographer to appreciate these visual delights, only to rise early or linger longer along the river's shoreline.

**81. Incense-cedar, Autumn Foliage.** The banks of the Merced River provide an ideal habitat for riparian shrubs and trees. Dogwoods, maples, cottonwoods and willows flourish throughout the summer but as days shorten and temperatures drop these deciduous trees begin their annual show of fall color.

**82. Fog and Forest Floor.** Autumn showers, fallen conifer needles and sunrise light combine to create an ethereal setting. Changes in weather can create sudden alterations of the surrounding forest. Fog rises from the river and colors become more intense transforming an ordinary scene into a chimerical one.

**83. Reflections and Maple Leaves.** The summit of El Capitan rises 3,245 feet above Yosemite Valley, the equivalent of three Empire State Buildings stacked one atop the other. Its granite is hard and forms the world's largest exposed monolith. Due to its height and strength 'The Captain' challenges climbing skills of hundreds each year.

**85. Sunset, El Capitan.** This stoic monolith has been called by many names through the centuries. The First People named ti 'To-to-konoo-lah', Sandhill Crane, after an early chief and Chief Tenaya's people called it 'To-tock-ah-noo-lah', Rock Chief. Another legend calls it 'Tul-tok-a-nula', measuring worm, while early settlers called it 'Crane Mountain'. It was the Mariposa Battalion, in 1851, who translated 'Rock Chief' to El Capitan. Regardless of what name it has been called, this icon will always command ones respect and admiration.

**86. Olmsted Point, Clearing Storm.** This magnificent viewpoint was named in honor, and appropriately so, of Fredrick Law Olmsted. Mr. Olmsted, co-designer of New York's Central Park, was lured to Mariposa to manage the bankrupt estate of John C. Fremont. While here he became interested in the future of nearby Yosemite. Olmsted accepted the post as Chairman of the first Board of Commissioners of the newly created park in 1864. His skills and foresight led to the unofficial title of 'the father of landscape architecture'.

**87. Last Light, Yosemite Valley.** Rapidly shifting light is the most visible change visitors see from the western end of Yosemite Valley. Geologically speaking, Yosemite appears to be ageless and unchanging, yet time and its agents are still at work reshaping the Park. Water, wind and ice are the prominent elements in precipitating these changes.

**88. Skier at Sunset.** We leave you with the warm glow of sunset streaking across Yosemite's high country, hoping your visit to Yosemite National Park has left you with pleasant memories and the desire to return and admire it again and again.

## PHOTOGRAPHER CREDITS

Jeff Nicholas:3,8,13,16,17,19,20,21,22,26,29,32,33,36,37,39,40, 43,45,47,55,56,58,59,60,66,68,72,74,76,77,78,79,80,84
Jim Wilson: 10,11,12,14,15,18,24,25,35,27,28,30,34,35,46,48,49, 54,57,61,62,64,69,70,71,75,81,82,85,87
Lewis Kemper: 42,44,51a,51b
Jeff Grandy: Cover,38,65,73
Chris Falkenstein: 51c,53,88
Annette Bottaro-Walklet: 63
Keith Walklet: 83
Dan Warsinger: 31
Walter Flint: 52
William Neill: 86
Michael Frye: 50

## BIBLIOGRAPHY

Arno, Stephen F.; Discovering Sierra Trees
    Yosemite Association, 1973

Botti, Stephen J. and Mendershausen, Ann;
    Wildflowers of the Hites Cove Trail
    Pioneer Publishing Co., 1985

Clarke, Charlotte Bringle;
    Edible and Useful Plants of California
    University of California Press, 1977

Morgenson, Dana C.;
    Yosemite Wildflower Trails
    Yosemite Association, 1975, 1988

Ditton Richard P. and McHenry, Donald E.;
    Yosemite Road Guide
    Yosemite Association, 1942, 1981

National Park Service;
    Guide to Yosemite High Sierra Trails
    Yosemite Association, 1987

National Park Service;
    Yosemite, Official National Park Handbook
    Division of Publications, U.S. Dept. of Interior

Schaffer, Jeffrey P.; Yosemite National Park
    Wilderness Press, 1978, 1983

Trexler, Keith A.; The Tioga Road, A History 1883-1961
    Yosemite Association, 1961, 1975, 1980

Wilson, Lynn and Jim, Nicholas, Jeffrey D.;
    Wildflowers of Yosemite
    Sierra Press Inc., 1987, 1990